DISCLAIMER

No part of this publication may be reproduced or distributed in any form or by any means, electronic or mechanical, or stored in a database or retrieval system without prior written permission from the author/publisher.

The author is not a licensed practitioner, physician or medical professional and offers no medical diagnoses, treatments, suggestions, or counseling. The information presented herein has not been evaluated by the U.S. Food and Drug Administration, and is not intended to diagnosis, treat, cure or prevent any disease. Full medical clearance from a licensed physician should be obtained before beginning or modifying any diet, exercise, or lifestyle program, and physicians should be informed of all nutritional changes.

The author/owner claims no responsibility to any person or entity for any liability, loss, or damage caused or alleged to be caused directly or indirectly as a result of the use, application, or interpretation of the information present herein.

ISBN: **979-8-9877563-1-7**

Graphics and Cover Design: **Bruce Schutter**

Author: **Bruce Schutter**

Editor: **Lee Schutter**

(V138 – KDP - Paperback)

I TRIUMPHED OVER BIPOLAR, ALCOHOLISM & ANXIETY DISORDER BY BECOMING A MENTAL HEALTH WARRIOR

Learn how you can become a Warrior and triumph over your life's challenges!

Bruce Schutter

TABLE OF CONTENTS

How to become a Mental Health Warrior

Warrior Component #1 - Creed

Warrior Component #2 - Values

Warrior Component #3 - Mindset Rules

Warrior Component #4 – Mental Health Warrior Tools

REAL-LIFE RESULTS

WARRIOR SECRETS

NOW, GO FORTH AND TRIUMPH

FOREWORD

Welcome to the Possibilities

Challenges in life come in many shapes and forms, in many sizes and all levels of importance but they have one common trait... they all want to control the direction of our day and our life! They are relentless in this pursuit and often leave us feeling defeated as our actions each day lead us nowhere. Resigned, we decide to settle and give up because we are powerless!

But it is not true! Our first line of action is within ourselves!

By becoming a Mental Health Warrior, we are prepared for the full range of challenges and emotions that life throws at us on a daily basis. With that power we will then triumph over our life's challenges and control the direction of our life.

Yeah, not those challenges that we see coming from 5 miles away, but the ones that come out of the clear blue sky and knock us right on our butts. The job that disappeared, the financial struggle from those unexpected expenses, or something simple like a flat tire that put us in such a foul mood, that when we got home, we made some really, really bad decisions! Or that unexpected feeling of depression that becomes a full-blown mental health challenge. Yes, the list goes on and on! But the one certainty is allowing our Life's Challenges to control the direction of our life is a really bad idea with bad results guaranteed.

But when we become a Mental Health Warrior, we start by learning to "Bend Not Break" under the weight of our challenges and the accompanying emotions. That allows us to remain firmly in control of the direction of our day and begin to take back the control that we have relinquished to our life's challenge. This is the first step to your New Life.

So read on with an open mind, learn to laugh again and embrace the power found in becoming a... **Mental Health Warrior!**

Mental Health is often only discussed

in the darkness,

yet it is intimately involved in shaping

every facet of our Life and

our Happiness.

Bring it to the light and

Unlock the power of a New Mindset,

Experience the excitement of a New Life,

Embrace all the possibilities of a New Future!

...Bruce

Mental Health Warrior - Unlimited Possibilities

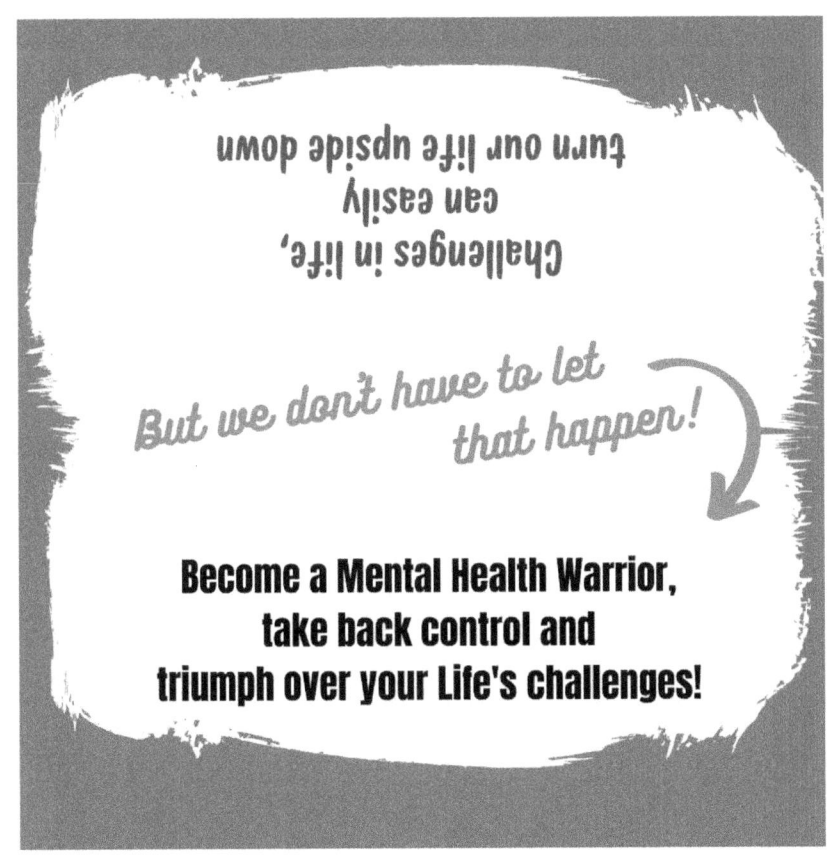

Challenges in life,
can easily
turn our life upside down

But we don't have to let
that happen!

Become a Mental Health Warrior,
take back control and
triumph over your Life's challenges!

MEET BRUCE

I was Unqualified for Daily Life

Join me for a brief tale, not of woe, but of learning lessons the hard way! For eventually I learned a lot of lessons in life, but I think they will have more meaning if you understand where they came from!

Something's Off

Throughout my teen and high school years, in the back of my head I always knew something was different. I only seemed to know the extremes of emotion and energy. Part of me just figured that was just how I was "wired" and funny enough that thought was not entirely wrong when I was diagnosed, much, much later with Bipolar II disorder.

That helps explain the emotions and energy, massive highs and lows. But what of the other symptoms… extreme anxiety, stressful situations where I found drinking helped me cope and the ever-present belief that whatever I did was not enough, especially to myself. Once again, answers to these questions came much later through diagnosis after diagnosis. But more on that later.

The Rescue Squad

During high school (10th -12th grade) I joined the local volunteer rescue squad with several of my friends. I began as a "support tech", then got certified as an "Emergency Medical Technician" (EMT-B) and even qualified to drive the ambulance. I immediately became hooked on the excitement, the true life-or-death situations, of which there were many!

For some reason, during the shifts and overnights, my crew and I always experienced plenty of calls. We responded to accidents, anywhere and of every imaginable outcome. Meaning we experienced results so traumatic, like being on scene and tending to an accident involving kids from a neighboring high school, where several of them died at the scene despite our best efforts and I still remember every detail today. I also experienced so many calls where I performed CPR, that I stopped counting after 20 times. Overall, everyone in the entire volunteer group experienced amazing saves and tragic endings. But unfortunately, we all had no training in how to process these events and were left to our own devices. This certainly was the start of both my depending on alcohol to numb feelings and the beginnings of developing a terrible mental health state.

For I had missed that while Life does contain bad things, we should learn to appreciate every day and make the most of that gift. But I kept always moving, probably due to mania, but it only served to keep me from seeing my problems in totality.

School (issues and issues)
I attended college, was massively involved in many, many of the social activities, campus groups, a fraternity and unfortunately, also beset by a host of situations where my performance was less than stellar. Let's just leave it at this for now.

Well, that is not fair, as my many "adventures" due to untreated alcoholism and unknown Bipolar thinking provided a mix of huge ups and downs. I certainly persevered and kept moving but with no real direction, for I still never really looked inward. But I graduated from college with a degree in Information Technology and worked as a Systems Analyst (ironically reviewing systems and finding better ways for them to operate).

Adventures on a Grand Scale
After being in the corporate workforce for 7 years, I got married and jumped into a whole new series of "adventures". This was adventures, misadventure, highs, and lows on a whole new adult scale. Such as buying a house, then buying investment real estate, and working on managing said properties. We also became avid antique collectors, which morphed into running small antique booths as a side business. Along the way, my adult job allowed us to purchase cars and of course only one would never do.

Just like hobbies that you cannot afford when younger, that now are available. But of course, in reality I could not truly afford everything, which leads to more stress and the days melt into each other. The idea was to keep busy with successes, or at least the appearance of success.

Now, don't get me started on how many things we could not truly afford but found complicated financial ways to borrow from a property to fund a new venture and then shift gear or focus a few months later. Think of a grander scale and even grander failures! This continued for 8+ years. But like any person truly lost in their problems, I used the same tired, well-worn methods to handle this lifestyle. (Plus, spoiler, you can NOT buy away your troubles.)

Problems Build & Build
This methodology also contributed to my losing physical strength, gaining weight, experiencing health problems (anxiety, stress, high BP, high cholesterol), being unable to find happiness in my accomplishments (negative mental health) and additional problems far too numerous to even summarize. But of course, it goes without saying that everything was reaching a peak and life was out of control, even when the illusion was maintained to the audience that I was handling everything! (Whew, it is even exhausting to just write all of that, LOL)

And Then Build Some More
Now my life consisted of the "normal" things between all of those other distractions I listed in the previous paragraphs. For I had several overnight visits to local police stations, several involuntary weekend commitments to psych facilities, many, many lost weekends, and all kind of mind-blowing situations… like where I had to get my car repaired from damage in hitting our other cars in our driveway… I mean all the normal background stuff, right? No! But still I continued, repeating the same tired solutions, and getting even worse results. Not even the same crappy results but worse results.

…PLEASE CONTINUE WITH ME

I Eventually Find the Solution

It Almost Ends

At this point I was stuck in the circle of alcoholism and mental health challenges for 20+ years. I remained firmly rooted in the circle despite the occasional rally to escape, which provided a brief respite but never realized the goal of long-term success. I became accustomed to the shame, the depression, the manic behavior, and the craziness of my life. You might even say that I reveled in the excitement on the surface. But I was deeply unhappy, going nowhere with my life as I could not find anything that inspired me or provided lasting happiness.

Now some of this was the result of my alcohol addiction, some a result of my Bipolar Brain and the rest was just the result of ignoring my Mental Health, letting all of the other mental health challenges I have run with abandon. Eventually this pushed me to the brink and a desperate roll of the dice… live or die attempt and let us suffice it to say, that I no longer wanted any part of this world. But luckily that was not to be my fate!

Start to Rebuild

But I still needed guidance, a direction for my life and basically needed to build everything from the ground up. That is really what changed the direction of my life…finding myself and what I am all about, my values. Or more accurately, what I wanted to be about, as I was so far from the person that I wanted to be. Which also left me very far away from happiness.

Open to Solutions

The day I decided I had had enough of challenges running my life, I embraced the concept that I would try out any solution and see if it could help me change my life. I feel that is an important first step, for we should not go into things without 100% commitment. That does not mean we cannot pivot throughout our journey as we find what works and does not work for our lives. But it simply means that we remain committed to finding a new way of living. Far from the circle of life's challenges running the show! Trust me, that simple pledge of commitment is an amazing first step, even when we have no idea what the path will look like.

Traditional Solutions

Once I made that commitment, I went to doctors, tried numerous medications for my bipolar, my generalized anxiety disorder (which loosely translates into extreme worry over everything) and of course meds for my poor health conditions (high BP, overweight, prediabetic, etc.). Basically, as I am sure you can tell I was a complete mess! But that was just part of what I tried, for I had committed to checking out everything.

I went to numerous therapists, I attended a large number of self-help groups and even read every book that I could find on the subject of alcoholism and mental health. Each avenue offered help, but when it was just me and the day, I crumbled. I would find myself reverting to old behaviors and could not sustain any progress on my new way of living.

Side Effects

Now most of the meds I tried had side effects, some minor annoyances, while others sent shocks throughout my body throughout the day leaving me almost unable to function. I also experienced the need for one medication to calm my mania and another to fight the depression that would creep in.

If you have been on any medications for mental health challenges, then I am sure that you are familiar with this journey that I am briefly speaking about. Eventually I did find a combination of meds that provided me enough stability so that I could think and that was a blessing. But again, when it was just me and the day, I crumbled as I had no solid plan for handling everyday challenges in life.

Still Struggling

I also still faced the challenge of how not to drink all the time as that was my go-to solution for the stressors of daily life. So, I went to therapists and to self-help groups. It was great to connect with someone, spill out all my troubles and gain a brief respite. But after leaving sessions or meetings, my newfound peace was quickly challenged by life, as that is just how life goes…there will always be challenges.

Eventually I realized that I needed to build some type of foundation in order to accept the help offered and make use of it outside of the sessions and meetings.

My Solution

My first thought was the one constant in my life is that I am always there. Yeah, I know, you may say "duh" at this point but stick with me for here comes the "big flip." If I am always present, then there must be a way for me to have an impact on my life's direction. **I realized that my Mental Health was at the core of everything**.

We make hundreds of decisions a day and they each have an impact on the direction of our life. But when they are made as simply reactions to challenges or by abdicating that power to challenges in life, then we have a problem! Our life goes nowhere, and we remain far from the life we want.

But when we become a Mental Health Warrior, our decisions can be made from a point of strength and clarity of thought. Now that makes logical sense, and I knew I was on to something extremely important. "If we remain in control of our life throughout any challenge, then it will go in the direction that we choose."

The Plan

I focused my energy each day on the Solution of becoming a Mental Health Warrior. That translated into each day learning to manage my emotions and become comfortable in them. This allowed me to stay in control of the day. I know that I am repeating this concept, but it is an important part of the process. For that life I had in the back of my mind all of those years was becoming a reality as each day I worked on the solution and was able to "Bend and Not Break" when confronted with challenges/emotions in life. <u>This meant I was firmly in charge of the direction of my life and progress was made.</u>

I think you see that turning point, I was becoming qualified to live life! I no longer worried about minor challenges but began to feel confident in my abilities to handle each "day." Now you may say what is so damn hard about getting through the day. But that is just my point… No longer did I just get through the day, I lived each day!

For the first time in a very long time, I took an active role in the day, enjoyed the challenges and when the sun would set… I was not filled with regret or a longing to escape…

I Lived Life!

The New Path

At this point I began to build the life I really wanted! For no longer was I under the power of life's challenge. I took control of the direction of my day and my life by being a Mental Health Warrior.

My life is still filled with challenges, because they are part of life, but I am in control, and I am ME! …and that is Awesome!

That is where my journey has brought me and I really, really want to share with everyone that you can…

Become a Mental Health Warrior

and

Triumph over any of Life's challenges!

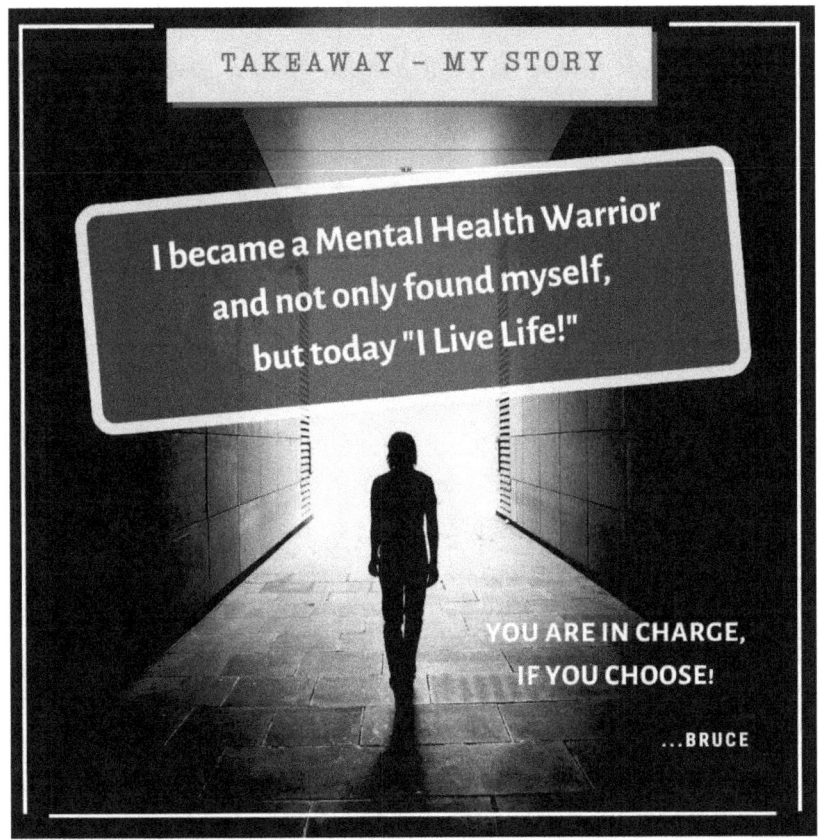

Bring on tomorrow,

for I no longer dread the Sunrise

but look forward with unparalleled Enthusiasm

for the Challenges of the Day!

Bruce Schutter

ACE – Certified Health Coach

ACE – Behavior Change Specialist

NASM – Certified Personal Trainer

Precision Nutrition – Certified Nutrition Coach

PN – Certified Sleep, Stress Management and Recovery Coach

MENTAL HEALTH WARRIOR EACH AND EVERY DAY

If Life came with credentials, this is me...

BRUCE

Recovering Alcoholic with a
Bipolar Mind (racing thoughts, deep depression)
and Anxiety Disorders (severe worry & stress over everything)!

**I triumphed over my life's challenges by becoming
a Mental Health Warrior**

I NOW EMBRACE THESE LABELS, BELIEVE IN MYSELF
AND LOVE MY UNIQUE WAY OF THINKING!

Mental Health Warrior Each and Every Day

LIFE LESSONS LEARNED

THE CONCLUSION

Mental Health is Important!

Mental Health is Important because
Life Equals Emotions

Yes, that is a simple statement, but wow, it will knock your socks off! For found within those three words is the essence of the solution to triumph over our life's challenges. I personally tried hundreds of solutions to help with my life challenges of Alcoholism, Bipolar, Anxiety disorders… but they always ended up falling short.

The Question
Why you ask? Most of the time I realized it was the emotions that come with everyday challenges that I could not manage. And don't get me started on the emotions that come with bigger scope life challenges. With those I immediately ran back to old behaviors to seek short lived comfort.

But finally, I saw the solution. I needed to get comfortable with the full spectrum of emotions that life contains and only then could I take the steps needed to triumph over my life's challenges.

The Answer
Now I know you may be skeptical at first, just like I was. For my Bipolar emotions lead me all over the map throughout the day, so how could they be part of the answer. But think back to the times you tried to get a handle on your life's challenges. Perhaps you veered into depression or felt the pressure of life and chose alcohol. The problem is not what challenge you have, but what keeps pushing us back to seek out those short-term solutions.

I found it was my emotions! If the pressure got to me, it was because I had no way to be comfortable in and manage that emotion. If I made a mistake, I would have no comfort with my emotions and could never see the lessons they were providing. My answer was to leave everything unaddressed in life. Soon every day is just filled with reasons to let my life's challenges pick the solutions. Wow, that is, and was, BAD!

But then I became a Mental Health Warrior and embraced a new way of living in which emotions play an important role in helping me see the beauty of the day while also propelling me forward in life. By learning about myself in the process, I have come to understand that our challenges can actually be something positive.

For when we learn to be comfortable in the full spectrum of emotions in life, we can ally with them. Now that is a powerful partnership, and I found the best way to describe it in this simple statement:

"My Emotions Broke Me, My Emotions Healed Me"

I know you can experience the same results, so please join me today in making your Mental Health a priority, as Life Equals Emotions.

...Bruce

THE SOLUTION

Mental Health + Warrior

WE BEGIN WITH THE WORD "MENTAL HEALTH"

Mental Health, the word itself seems to elicit only two responses from people. Either they suddenly get very quiet and almost begin to whisper as they talk about some type of mental health challenge, and we should all be filled with sorrow for even mentioning it.

…or, it is about a crazy over-the-top idea for how to be happy every minute of your life. But those responses are a far cry from the true powers represented by the word Mental Health, which encompasses the full spectrum of emotions and our ability to be comfortable with them.

NEXT, WE ADD IN THE WORD "WARRIOR"

Now Warrior is a unique word that can be applied to many areas of our life, but the best definition I found is both simple and powerful… someone with the ability to **"Bend Not Break!"**

What a display of true strength as we imagine a tree bending, creaking and swaying in the middle of hurricane force winds but never crashing to earth.

RESULT: MENTAL HEALTH WARRIOR

Now when we combine "Mental Health" with "Warrior", that is where the magic occurs. We learn to ally with our emotions, unlock the power to triumph over our life's challenges and build the life we really want.

One where we, not our life's challenges, are firmly in control of the direction of our day and life. Now that is a powerful and life-changing solution. One that is available to everyone, for we all have the power within ourselves to become Mental Health Warriors.

Today is the day
You = Mental Health Warrior

GOOD NEWS

**Become a Mental Health Warrior
and you can change the direction of your Life!**

BAD NEWS

**It will take work... sorry,
"NO FREE LUNCH"**

...but the results are delicious!

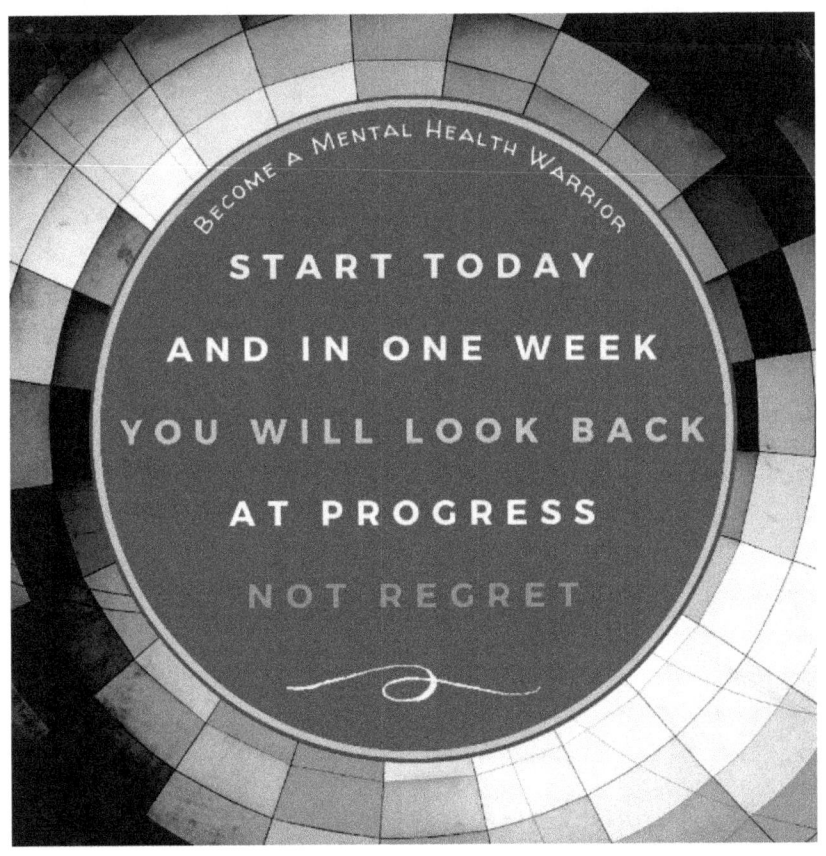

STILL NOT CONVINCED

(Stats to Ponder)

Personal Note:
This section of the book requires a bit of seriousness and formality. No, not like the 1800's when everyone wore a suit, or at least that's what I infer from movies, as I was not there.

But because I can tell you just from my small foray into the world, that people's Mental Health has tremendous impact on their lives, both good and bad. It is often the lynchpin that determines which course of action they will take when confronted with the truly serious challenges of life. So, for a few minutes let's put aside the humor and just take in the numbers.

One last word… **if you feel, like me, that you are part of these numbers then be assured, there is a solution and a way out!**

…Bruce

(Stats to Ponder)

Do Not Feel Ashamed

"In order to love who you are, you cannot hate the experiences that shaped you." - Andrea Dykstra

Not Alone in Our Problems

NAMI/NIMH Stats (2019)

19.1% of U.S. adults experienced <u>mental illness</u> in 2018 (47.6 million people). This represents 1 in 5 adults.

4.6% of U.S. adults experienced <u>serious</u> mental illness in 2018 (11.4 million people). This represents 1 in 25 adults.

16.5% of U.S. youth aged 6-17 experienced a mental health disorder in 2016 (7.7 million people)

3.7% of U.S. adults experienced a co-occurring substance use disorder and mental illness in 2018 (9.2 million people)

Less than 43% of adults will get treatment.

Everyone at some point in their life will experience a Mental Health crisis or experience.

Ripple Effect

- People with serious mental health illness have an increased risk for chronic disease
- Each year, serious **mental illness costs** Americans $193 billion in lost earnings, finds a study in the May American Journal of Psychiatry (Vol. 165, No. 5)

(Stats to Ponder)

Anxiety

- According to the **Anxiety and Depression Association of America**, anxiety disorders are the most common mental illness in the U.S.
- Anxiety affects 40 million adults age 18 and older, or roughly 18.1% of the population
- Although anxiety disorders are highly treatable, only 36.9% of those suffering receive treatment.

Chronic Anxiety

Results in prolonged flood of Adrenaline & Cortisol, resulting in continued physical responses (heart rate increased, muscle tension, sweating) which is not good for health and results in:

- Heart conditions - due to HR being increased.
- High BP - also due to faster HR
- Asthma or not calm breathing
- Gastrointestinal problems - due to heightened anxiety
- Insomnia - due to being keyed up.
- Blood Sugar Spikes - liver produces more glucose to boost energy.
- Weight gain - due to stress eating
- Muscle tension - results in clenching, leads to headaches or jaw pain.

Depression

- Major depression is one of the most common mental health disorders in America, according to the **National Institute of Mental Health**
- Depression affects 350 million people worldwide.
- 16 million American adults reported having at least one major depressive episode in 2015

19% of Adults with a Mental Health Illness have a Substance Use Disorder

Sobering Numbers - Suicide

- 2nd leading cause for death for ages 10-34
- Overall Suicide rate has increased 313% since 1999
- Suicide is the 10th leading cause of death in the US

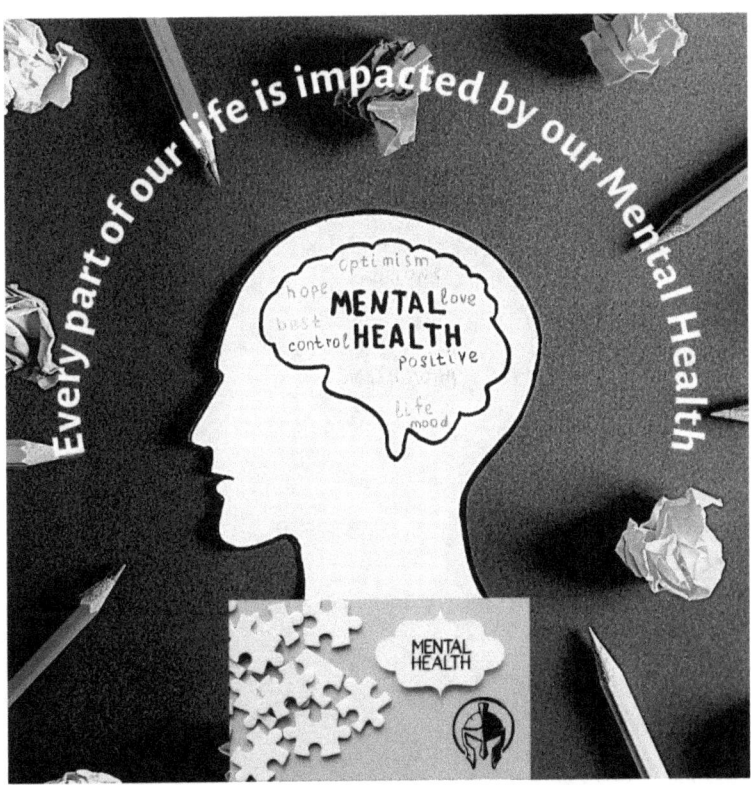

BENEFITS OF BEING A WARRIOR

MENTAL HEALTH WARRIOR
BENEFIT #1

Comfortable with the Full Spectrum of Emotions

The Mental Health Warrior is comfortable with and able to manage the full spectrum of emotions that life contains. Yes, even those that we wish were not there! For we are stuck with them as they are part of the "Life Package."

Which even on its worst day it is much, much better than that other "Not-life Package!"

So, rather than fighting our emotions and wishing we were a robot, instead we learn to be comfortable with experiencing them. Then we can learn to Respond Not React and make choices that will keep us moving forward in the direction that we choose.

This is an awesome example of the skills we develop as a Warrior that will help us change our life.

Mental Health Warrior
...where I experience my emotions but
they no longer break me,
as I am comfortable in the full spectrum of emotions!

For truth be told,
Emotions are never meant for the background,
but rather they bring the sharpness and clarity
to each day and every experience!

Never let them play a secondary role
in your life!

...Bruce

MENTAL HEALTH WARRIOR
BENEFIT #2

Power to triumph over Life's Challenges

Being comfortable with our emotions is a great start but it also feels kinda limited. It is like being in your recliner, favorite show on the tv and the remote in your hand, just in case. But then hunger strikes and all the willpower in the world will not levitate a snack from the fridge into your hands.

Now even in this corny example, we cannot stop a challenge from occurring, but if we remain in control, we can manage the challenge and continue on our chosen path for the day. In this case that means not getting upset, placing the show on pause, and making that long trek to the kitchen, LOL!

Go ahead and chuckle! But that is actually the same path we will follow to triumph over the most serious of life's challenges. We become a Mental Health Warrior which enables us to pause when challenged and then choose a response that keeps us on the course we choose.

Empowered, we triumph over life's challenges by never relinquishing control of the direction of the day and thus our life.

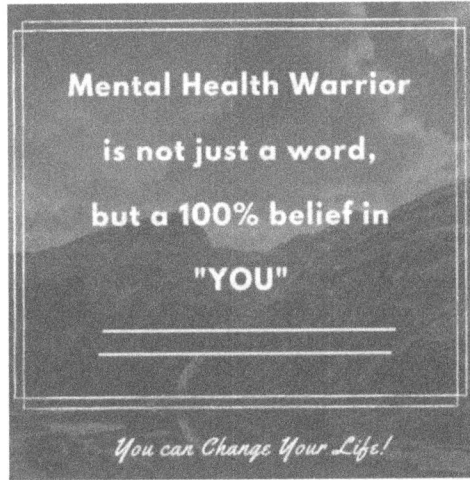

- 55 -

MENTAL HEALTH WARRIOR
BENEFIT #3

Sustainability

Now it would be amazing if we could simply defeat a challenge today and know it never resurfaces. But life's challenges are not that simple and often reappear unexpectedly, as that is one of the ways they work to exert their control over our life. But we no longer have to fear these occurrences, as a Mental Health Warrior is the embodiment of sustainability.

Which loosely translates into the fact that "we are always prepared for the next challenge!" So, rest assured, when you become a Warrior and a new challenge rears its head… you will be prepared and no longer fear any of your emotions.

Be wary of quick definitions,

for only when we understand the

complexities and meaning of a word,

can we begin to embrace its power in our Life.

EACH AND EVERY DAY!

MENTAL HEALTH + WARRIOR

BENEFITS:

(1)
Comfortable with the
Full Spectrum of Emotions
in Life

(2)
Power to Triumph over
Life's Challenges

(3) Sustainability (always ready for the next challenge)

MENTAL HEALTH WARRIOR

How to become a
Mental Health Warrior

WARRIOR COMPONENT #1

CREED

WARRIOR'S - CREED

"Bend Not Break"

POWER OF THE
CREED

POWER OF THE CREED

"Bend Not Break"

Cool warrior creed, you say, but the real question is does it work in real life? Well, the answer is a resounding Yes! For it embodies an approach that will work with all levels of challenges in life and is always available as it comes from within ourselves. Those two factors are what make this approach so powerful in it addresses the core reason we have often failed in the past and guides us to success today.

Lose Fear of Emotions

But as a warrior armed with the creed of "Bend Not Break", we embrace an entirely new way of living. One in which we become comfortable in the full spectrum of emotions. Which means when they arise, we will no longer be stopped in our tracks but will be able to understand them. That is an important first step in our journey as we turn our warrior creed into real-life action.

Stop Relinquishing Control

Next, as we no longer fear emotions, we can use an almost unlimited array of tools to help us Bend Not Break as we skillfully navigate through both our emotions and challenges. Understanding that progress throughout the day equals success. For it does not matter how many times you had to regroup to handle a situation or the number of tools you needed to use. The key to success is to never relinquish control of your day to our challenge and therefore stay on the course that you set for your life.

No Longer Breaking

That is the true power of the warrior creed, and it made all the difference in my ability to triumph over my personal life challenges of alcoholism, bipolar and anxiety disorders. For instead of letting my emotions break me or send me scurrying back to old behaviors, I now find myself able to take the steps needed to make forward progress in my life.

Plus, as a warrior I am always prepared for the next challenge and thus always moving forward. That is the powerful approach available to us with the Warrior Creed of **"Bend Not Break!"**

A Warrior often delights us with more than
their sheer strength or power.

We delight in seeing the football player run,
weave their way past the tackles,
brushing off the contacts and
ending up in the end zone.

We are delighted by seeing James Bond,
captured but then escaping,
again and again from the traps of the evil villain, eventually
saving the world.

We also feel pride in our own demonstrations of
being a warrior when challenged,
when even with our backs-to-the-wall,
we emerge successfully from life's challenges.

It is apparent that the sheer delight of a Warrior
lies in the ability to manage the
situations and our emotions,
rather than the pain we experience from
running headfirst into walls.

...Bruce

WARRIOR CREED
VS.
MY LIFE'S CHALLENGES

Mental Health Warrior Creed vs.
My Life's Challenges

Alcoholism

For me drinking was a way to escape from my emotions, as I was not comfortable with them and as a result was completely unprepared to manage them. I eventually relinquished control of the direction of my life to life's challenges... Not a good result anyway you look at it!

But becoming a Mental Health Warrior offered a solution. A new way of living where I no longer fear my emotions but embrace them as they no longer have the power to drive me back to short term solutions like drinking.

Today I Bend Not Break when challenges and the accompanying emotions arise. This allows me to remain firmly in control of the direction of the day and I can take the steps needed to triumph each day over my alcohol addiction. That is the proof of the creed in action!

"If I can do it, You Can Too"

Bipolar Disorder

Bipolar is all about emotions, the extreme highs and the devastating lows that take away all hope. It is also a never-ending cascade of these emotions that can be exhausting and cause us to relinquish control of our life to Life's Challenges... with really disastrous results!

But when I became a... Mental Health Warrior I found another option. A new way of living where I embrace the full spectrum of emotions in life by knowing I have the power to bend not break whenever they arise. This has allowed me to understand that they are part of my story, and they show me the true heights & depths of life.

The biggest difference today is that when my emotions swing to the ends of the spectrum, I no longer fear this, but instead have the tools, including the approach built with the warrior creed, which allows me to manage my emotions. Today I am confident and no longer under the control of my bipolar disorder.

"Fear Leaves, when we have the tools to Face It!"

Anxiety Disorders

I found the best description for my anxiety disorder is that I simply stress and worry about everything! The result was I lost all belief in myself and my decisions, eventually relinquishing control of my day to this life challenge.

If you find common ground in these thoughts, then becoming a Mental Health Warrior offers a solution. I use Warrior Weapons to challenge these fears and discover they are often hollow. But when they are justified, I understand that we all have times of anxiety and stress.

This combination allows me to no longer be subject to anxiety's control. Instead, armed with my warrior weapons I am now, and remain, in control of the direction of my life.

"Anxiety Lies, but today we see the Truth"

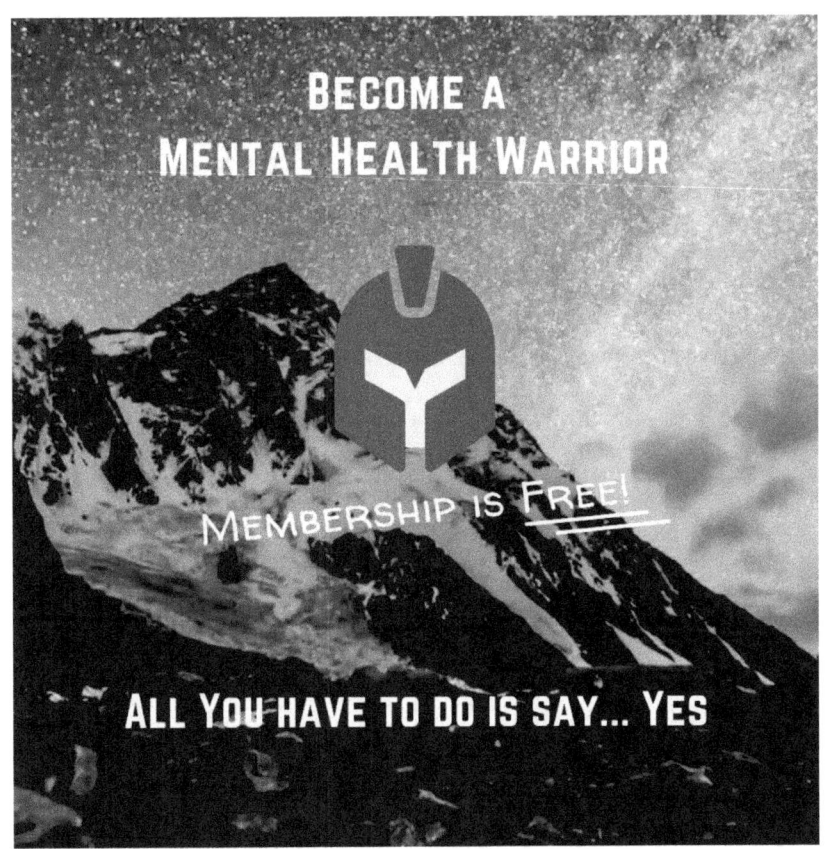

WARRIOR COMPONENT #2

VALUES

WHAT ARE VALUES?

What are Warrior's Values?

As a Mental Health Warrior, values serve as the compass, guiding one through the complexities of emotions, challenges, and triumphs. The second crucial component of the Mental Health Warrior's arsenal is Values, and they play a dual role in shaping a new, purposeful life.

Role #1 - Setting the Direction for Goals and Pursuits

Values are not mere abstract concepts; they are the pillars that uphold the structure of your goals and aspirations. As a Mental Health Warrior, defining your values in various areas of life becomes paramount. It's a two-fold process: identifying your goals and determining the values that will drive you toward those objectives.

These goals could span a spectrum—professional ambitions, expertise in specific areas, or indulging in hobbies that ignite your passion. What you define as valuable in these pursuits becomes the guiding force for a Mental Health Warrior. It provides direction in managing emotions and overcoming challenges. When your daily actions align with these values, each step becomes a purposeful stride towards increased happiness and fulfillment.

Role #2 - Defining How You Want to Live

The second facet of values is perhaps even more profound—it involves defining how you want to live your life. This decision is pivotal, especially when faced with challenges such as mental health disorders. As a Mental Health Warrior, it's about taking control and consciously choosing the path you want to tread.

For instance, in my journey, it meant deciding not to let mental health challenges dictate the terms of my life. This part of values extends to broader life choices, such as my choosing sobriety. By valuing sobriety, you not only justify channeling your energy into living this way but also reap enormous rewards—control over your life and pride in choosing your path.

Understanding and defining values in both goal-oriented pursuits and lifestyle choices is the cornerstone of the warrior's journey, as they clearly set the direction for our new life.

<u>**Or Simply Stated:**</u>

By identifying what we Value...

We establish a clear direction for our Warrior Path!

<u>**My Experience - It's Exciting!**</u>

I personally found this first step brought a level of clarity to my life that I never had before. Previously, I spent most of my time each day reacting to the numerous challenges of the day. Many of them were caused by me reacting badly because my crystal ball was always broken. No, actually it was perpetually cloudy, and it usually kept me locked into a circle of actions. Where I was always busy but ended up going nowhere!

But then I took the time to discover and identify what I valued in life. Most of what I found were not physical items but ideals on how I want to live and the goals I wanted to reach. But nonetheless, they remained far out of reach, until I took time to get honest with myself and commit to them.

Now that is when it got exciting! And I do mean exciting, like skiing straight down the Himalayas. – No, No, that is a terrible visual... please erase that last sentence from your mind and fill in something where you do not end up stuck in a big snowball forever.

Instead think about those things you have pushed into the back reaches of your mind and imagine bringing them out into the daylight. Now that is exciting and just the start of identifying what you value, which will set the direction for your new life.

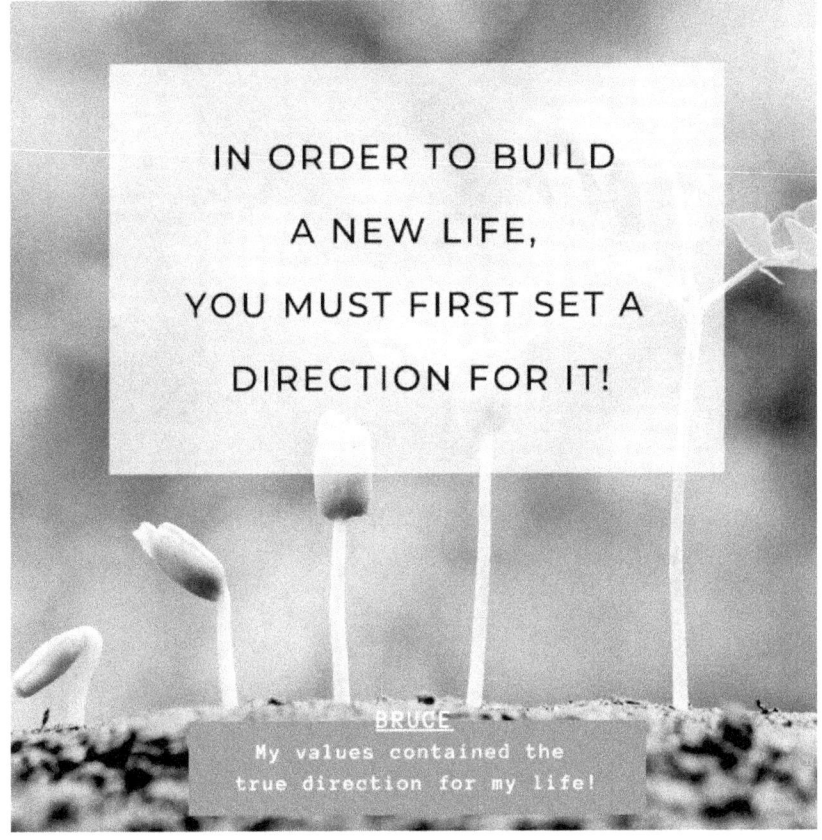

IN ORDER TO BUILD

A NEW LIFE,

YOU MUST FIRST SET A

DIRECTION FOR IT!

BRUCE
My values contained the
true direction for my life!

THE POWER OF

VALUES

The Power of Values

Identifying your Values is the first step in your journey, and I believe the best way to underscore their importance is to…

Demonstrate the power that Values have in your life!

They set the Direction for Actions

The things that we value, such as time with friends, achieving work in certain fields or simply a bike ride in the park, all play a role in setting the direction for the choices we make in life. But it is not enough to identify our values, like the examples above. We make sure that our choices each day support these values.

Think about it, if you never set time aside to meet up with friends you will never have time in your day to enjoy the activities with them. Instead, you find yourself in the park wondering where everyone is?! Not the outcome we want, but one we can avoid by staying true to our values.

So, let's check in with our values, say "hi" each day and then enlist their help in determining the direction of the day. Trust me, your values will not let you down, as they are found and set by you!

Plus, when we keep our actions aligned with them, then the day and our life will progress in the direction we control.

Put in the effort to determine your true values and you will be rewarded with each action you take!

Glue in Tough Times

The things that we value also serve us well in times of trouble. When life's challenges spin the day to the negative, we can find our way back by listening to our values.

Back in my previous life, I placed a lot of value on buying material goods and outlandish adventures. I mean who doesn't need to fly from New Hampshire to Chicago for the weekend as a reward for a really long work week. Or who doesn't need 5 cars sitting in their driveway because you feel that having a choice each day of what to drive is the path to happiness.

Yes, true stories for both and rest assured they were also things that I could not afford. But that is how lost I was in life and when it came crashing down… what led me out of the mess was my true values. I realized the folly of having 5 cars, both in terms of the cost and more importantly my time. For how I spent "my time" was now one of my primary values.

For, unless you have a time machine in your laundry room, we all get just 24 hours each day. Thus, where I spend that precious commodity needs to be on what I actually value, such as spending time with friends/family or learning a new skill.

I will let you in on a little secret… our whirlwind trips to Chicago, our shopping up and down the miracle mile never brought out the smile I get from enjoying a good horror movie, snacks (shared with our cats of course) and all in our 3-room apartment.

Because that represents time well spent and it can certainly pull me out of depression. That is a powerful result they provide to us as Mental Health Warriors.

Values in action have the power to rescue us in tough times!

Supports Personal Growth

Now this last one hit me like that smack on the back of the head from Special Agent Gibbs on the NCIS show. It jolted me awake and I found that our values grow with us as we become more comfortable in our new way of living.

For example, when I began building my new way of living, I was working in the Information Technology field. I initially planned to continue working in this area, but soon discovered that I valued something different. Initially this was scary as it was leading me into unknown waters! But then, bamm, it hit me…

New Me = New Values!

The fear was replaced as I rejoiced in a new path. Today I find myself writing a book about my story and the power of becoming a Mental Health Warrior. Wow, that is about as far from working in the IT field as I can imagine! But as my values grow with me, I find an immense amount of happiness in my day.

Embrace the growth of your values and they will provide never-ending support for your New Life!

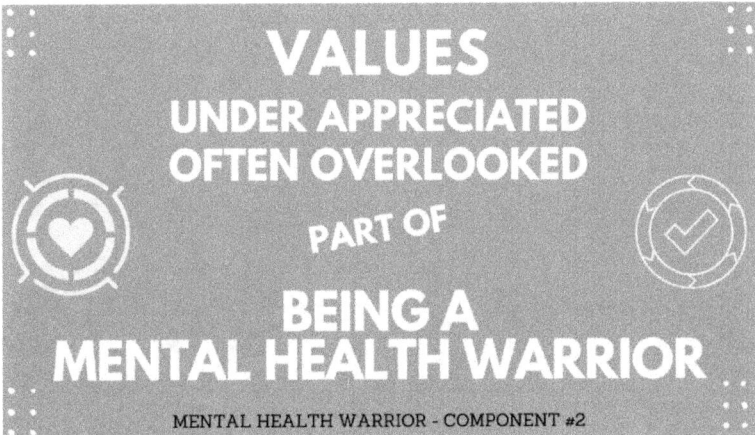

VALUES
UNDER APPRECIATED
OFTEN OVERLOOKED
PART OF
BEING A
MENTAL HEALTH WARRIOR
MENTAL HEALTH WARRIOR - COMPONENT #2

VALUES

Those things that we find in the furthest

reaches of our mind...

define who we want to be,

influence the direction of our life

and impart meaning to our actions!

...Bruce

DISCOVER YOUR VALUES

First a word of Caution!

I want to share with you a brief story to demonstrate why it is so important to be honest with yourself and dig deep when identifying our values.

Misidentified Values

After years of letting my life challenges run the show, I knew I needed to stop drinking and address my anxiety disorders, as my life was completely out of control. So, I quickly made them two of my values and started taking action to make them happen. But little did I know that my values were off, and I was headed down another bad road.

At this time, as the internet was exploding, I found that I could order valium on-line. Then when in the middle of work challenges and I felt my emotions getting the better of me, instead of drinking I could calm myself down with a little blue pill. Next, I rationalized that when I had a big meeting at work, which is stressful, it wouldn't hurt to take a little pill. Then at night, that same pill could keep me from drinking as it would calm me down and I would prevail over drinking. I thought I was putting my values into action.

I Succeed But Still Fail

Yes, technically I had achieved what I value… living without the crutch of drinking or giving into my anxiety disorders. But wow was I on the wrong path and it got so bad that I was almost lost to this world… literally!

Luckily, I am still here! But this is why I believe this first step to discovering our values is of critical importance! For if we make progress, but it is in the wrong direction, then we only end up far from the life we desire.

Now, let's start this journey of discovering our values with the honesty found in the… <u>Simulation Experience</u>!

THE
SIMULATION EXPERIENCE

Simulation Experience

TIME NEEDED:

10-20 minutes of undisturbed reflection time.

DESIRED OUTCOME:

Ensure what you Value is correctly defined as this is a critical starting point!

THE EXERCISE:

I want you to imagine that you wake up tomorrow and everything is gone. Poof! All of your possessions, your family, friends, job, etc.... everything has been taken from you by some mystical force or aliens! Yes, even those snacks you hid in your bedside table!

This exercise may seem odd but most people who have been in a serious accident or other near-death experiences, relate that afterwards, they realize that most things we worry about each day are in reality not that important. They also learn that by putting all our energy into worry, that we miss spending time on many of the truly important things in our life.

So, without the risk, we undertake this same exercise from the safety of your favorite chair. Then, we will use the results to jump start the building of your "values" list.

To keep it simple, you can only have 5 things in your life, so make sure that they are what is really, really important to you!

Examples

- My family as they make me happy, and I want to be part of their life.
- My job because I really enjoy working on my chosen career path and find personal satisfaction in meeting the challenges.
- A favorite hobby, such as bike riding or pursuing my hobby with like-minded friends.
- I want to regain control and stop letting depression or some other challenge in life set the direction for my life.

The 5 Things you Want Back:

_____

_____

_____

_____

_____

FINAL THOUGHTS:

While this may have seemed like a bizarre experiment… it should get you thinking and that is key! For our Values are the guideposts that channel our journey in the correct direction.

They are an all important first step in our journey of becoming a Mental Health Warrior and triumphing over Life's challenges!

Wait... Don't Forget "<u>You</u>"

Ok, as you build your list of values, take a quick moment and check... did you include yourself on the list? I bet you didn't!

<u>Common Mistake</u>
We often include family, friends and activities but we forget the basic fact... that if we do not take care of ourselves first, there will be no one to do those things. So do not fall for the common mistake of forgetting you must first be present in order to help others. You Count!

<u>Stop Old Habits</u>
When you add yourself to the list... you can stop old habits in their tracks! Today my choices are driven by my values and that is like entering the toll road, receiving the ticket, and selecting your exit in advance. That way you avoid the rash temptation of taking that exit to see the world's largest ball of twine, spending all day and then missing that job interview.

Not a good outcome (and in truth the ball of twine is really not that impressive.) I digress, but I am sure you get the point. If we know our destination up front, then we can keep the distractions or reverting to old behaviors to a minimum as they will just not help us get to our chosen destination.

<u>Not Selfish</u>
When your actions demonstrate your commitment to your new way of living... that more than justifies the time you spend on yourself! Yup, that simple. If you are aligning your actions with your values, you will do good things for yourself and those around you. What a great outcome!

You are an Important part of your life and others,
never forget this simple logic and
your values will be complete!

VALUES WRAP-UP

(Enjoy a Fun Analogy!)

The Map, The Boat, and The Weather

Ok, we are beginning to understand that our values are an extremely important part of our journey in becoming a Mental Health Warrior and triumphing over the challenges in our life. But life rarely follows a straight line and that is what makes it both so amazing and so challenging!

The Map

To better understand the role that our values play in being a Mental Health Warrior please join me for a quick analogy. Imagine we are going to explore the world, the first thing we will need is a map! This allows us to not only pick our destination but to also select the route to get there.

For just as there are hundreds of ways to get from point A-to-B on a map, there are many, many ways that we can make our values into reality. Plus, just like any good explorer, as soon as we get to the next point on the map, we will want to then get to point C and so on!

I relate this part of the analogy to many of my personal challenges, such as my Bipolar way of thinking. I am excited and eager to learn to avoid "falling off the cliff" into depression. But I always want to continue to explore life and find additional areas of happiness. So, I work to plot a course in life to avoid the deep pits of depression and explore other destinations in my life where I will find happiness. That will also coincidentally help keep me out of depression.

I understand my values provide help with both the destination and in determining the direction to take on the map.

The Boat

Now in order to do all of this exploring we will need a way to get there and as 71% of the earth is covered in water, we will need a boat! It provides us with the power to travel between our destinations and it also contributes to making the voyage enjoyable. Two important factors!

In our journey of building a new way of living, our boat is being a Mental Health Warrior. It will provide us with the power to travel to all our destinations. Now since I created this analogy, I acknowledge that it is impossible to sail the boat into the middle of Kansas, LOL!

But let's stretch the truth a bit and imagine our boat can sail on any tiny bit of water, even a small stream. So, we can get close enough to any destination that we will only have a short walk! In other words, being a Mental Health Warrior is an amazing boat that makes our journey possible!

It is also important to understand that the "quality" of our boat plays an important role in making each day of the journey enjoyable. Our Mental Health Warrior boat does an amazing job in that area. For not only can it help us get to our destination, but it allows us to triumph over the daily challenges so that we can enjoy each day.

For there is no better motivation than this to keep us going on our journey. For even the tough days, have bright spots of sunshine!

Our boat is both a powerful means of transportation as well as a large contributor to the enjoyment of the journey!

The Weather

We meticulously plan out our destination, the route we will take, stock the boat with supplies and then set off excitedly to take the journey. But then there is that uncontrollable factor in any exploration... the weather! While it may be out of our control, it will not stop us as we can use our resources to adjust the route and we have the supplies to make it happen.

Becoming a Mental Health Warrior built around our values, we can make the same adjustments in life. When we encounter a challenge that is out of our control, we simply revisit our values to reinforce the destination and keep our actions aligned with those values.

I find this happens a lot in my life, as although I no longer want to drink over my challenges, that does not mean they do not try to tempt me. As a recovering alcoholic, I am perhaps hyper aware of how many times alcohol is prompted in life. The ads in magazines, the characters drinking in movies, the offer of drinks in almost every menu... all challenges that like to pop in right out of the blue sky.

But I no longer fear these challenges, as I am a Warrior, and its powerful components safely see me through these challenges.

Even when a storm forms right out of the blue sky, I am always prepared for the weather, and it never deters me from my exploration of life.

On a personal note: I do white knuckle it through these challenges today, as I am so excited to be living life, that thought of giving up control of the day for a drink or other short-term solution, is a minor blip on the road, quickly passed by. That is the powerful result of me identifying my Values and becoming a Mental Health Warrior.

I hope you enjoyed this analogy and are excited to discover your values!

...Bruce

find what you **Value** and
you will look forward to
jumping out of bed
in the mornings...

actually, the whole day will
have **more meaning**

WARRIOR COMPONENT #3

MINDSET RULES

WHAT ARE
MINDSET RULES?

What are Mindset Rules?

Do not freak out, as these are not "rules" you have experienced in the past. Like the time-honored rule of stop eating 1 hour before you go swimming, or you will get cramps and drown. Which by the way is false, as when I was a lifeguard many summers ago, I actually ate a sandwich in the pool while swimming and did not drown. So, you can feel free to ignore that rule but that does NOT mean you can ignore Mindset Rules!

For each Mindset Rule reminds you of certain truths that often get lost in the hectic pace of today's world. And in turn this helps us keep our emotions centered throughout the day, so we do not relinquish control to our life's challenges!

So, embrace the philosophical nature of Mindset Rules and the powerful weapon they provide you as a Warrior.

Now if you feel the need to go to Tibet and become a monk to further the philosophical aspect of these rules, please share them with the Dalai Lama. I believe he will understand their importance and encourage their use as you grow to become a… Mental Health Warrior and embrace your New Life!

Key Takeaways:
- They offer both a proactive approach to manage stressors and are equally valuable as tools to guide you in effectively responding to challenges so you can move forward from them.

- This ensures that you, as a Mental Health Warrior, never relinquish control of the day to life's challenge but remain firmly in charge of each day.

10 "Starter" Mindset Rules

10 "STARTER" MINDSET RULES

(Guaranteed to Work - Batteries Not Required!)

#1 - Acknowledge the Importance of your Mental Health.

#2 - Respond Not React to Life's challenges.

#3 - Talk about It.

#4 - Build your Mental Health Toolbelt

#5 - Do Not expect or demand Perfection.

#6 - Forgive Yourself for Not Knowing
the things you Know Now.

#7 - Work on the things you can control
and let go of the rest.

#8 - Judge your Success by Your Plan and Not others.

#9 - Micro-steps.

#10 - Have Fun!

Say Hello
to your
Mindset Rules

SAY HELLO TO YOUR MINDSET RULES

#1 - Acknowledge the Importance of your Mental Health

When we acknowledge something, it then secures a place on our "what we value" list.

Therefore, the first step we take is to acknowledge to ourselves, that our Mental Health is an important part of our life. This is an essential first step in becoming a Mental Health Warrior.

#2 - Respond Not React to Life's Challenges

When we react to life's challenges, we tend to make choices in haste. This often leads to a response, dictated by the situation and that leaves a lot up to chance. Not what we want! Instead, we need to learn how to interject a brief pause, allowing ourselves time to think and then respond with an answer.

This does not mean that we cannot respond quickly only that today we take the time to keep everything in alignment with the direction that we choose! A subtle but important change in how we make choices!

#3 - Talk About It

This rule helps to make things real in our life, by translating feelings into words and bringing them out into the light of the day. They take on additional meaning and we can also share our experiences and thoughts with others.

This will allow us to help others as we build solutions to our life's challenges. This is an amazing experience that you will want to repeat and is also a powerful tool for developing solutions.

#4 - Build Your Mental Health Toolbelt

We prepare for life's curve balls by building a Mental Health Toolbelt. This is a series of Warrior Tools that you find work successfully in your life.

In turn we wear our toolbelt everywhere and therefore always have access to them. This ensures that we can always reach for the right tool when needed and can extract ourselves from whatever challenge life throws at us.

#5 - Do Not Expect or Demand Perfection

We need to make sure that we keep a realistic approach to life. Even when we are committed to such an important change, we must avoid unrealistic expectations.

Such as, that we will never have a bad day. This expectation will only invite unnecessary problems into our day, as no one is perfect, and mistakes will happen. Even when pursuing a noble goal such as changing the direction of your life, we can avoid this setback by reminding ourselves to set a realistic expectation!

#6 - Forgive Yourself for Not knowing the things you know Now

Many times, once we learn how to manage something in life, we then start to feel like we should have applied this knowledge to situations in the past. "I should have done this" is a common statement. But this is unrealistic as we cannot change the past and it minimizes our success.

This rule reminds us to not to penalize ourselves for something we did not know! Remain focused on the present and apply what you have learned, as that is where we can make changes!

#7 – Work on the things You Can Control and let go of the rest

As a Mental Health Warrior we will learn many ways to triumph over life's challenges, but there will still be parts of life that are out of our control. That is normal!

But as we cannot banish them from our life, we must learn to not fixate on these challenges, but remain focused on the results. That equals success and confirms that it is ok to let go what is out of our control!

#8 – Judge your Success by Your Plan Not others

It is always important to remember that as we become a Mental Health Warrior that we are also building **our plan**. One that is uniquely built to triumph over our life's challenges.

Therefore, we must remember to define success each day against our plan. Do not fall into the trap of measuring your day against what you see in the media or on tv… instead be true to yourself and celebrate making progress toward your goals each day!

#9 – Micro-Steps

Following the path of micro-steps (small improvement or task) each day is key to avoid being overwhelmed and still make progress each day.

Plus, these continual small successes will strengthen you as a Mental Health Warrior and provide you with the ability to handle challenges of increasing depth and complexity!

#10 - Have Fun!

Allow yourself some time to enjoy your new life. We did not decide to change our lives so we could spend all day working on problems. Instead, we become a Mental Health Warrior, triumph over Life's challenges, so that we have time to enjoy each day and its experiences.

Personally, having fun is one of the top rewards of my new life!

MINDSET RULES

GENTLE REMINDERS OF
CERTAIN TRUTHS

KEEP YOUR EMOTIONS
CENTERED
AND YOU IN CHARGE!

NEVER FORGET:
RULE #10 - HAVE FUN!

WARRIOR COMPONENT #4

MENTAL HEALTH WARRIOR TOOLS

What are Mental Health Warrior Tools?

What are Mental Health Tools?

DESCRIPTION:
"Mental Health Warrior Tools" are a collection of therapeutic techniques intricately woven into everyday activities, combining the power of self-care with the demands of daily life.

HOW DO THEY WORK?
First, it must be noted that the tools range in size, much like the challenges we face, from large too small. But they all contribute to being a Mental Health Warrior, where we Bend Not Break when faced with any level of life challenge and the accompanying emotions.

Think of the Mental Health Tools in the same way you would use a screwdriver. When you go to make lunch and find a loose door in your kitchen, you simply grab the screwdriver and tighten the hinges. Then you can continue with accomplishing the goal that brought you to the kitchen in the first place. MMM, Lunch!

Mental Health Tools are meant to be used in the same manner. When we encounter a challenge, without disrupting our entire day, we use the tool to triumph over the challenge and continue with the direction we set for the day. That approach will keep us moving forward as we have an almost unlimited number of tools that we can apply as a Mental Health Warrior to triumph over the challenges of the day!

Key Takeaways:
- These tools hold the unique ability to help us effectively manage our mental health and navigate challenges seamlessly while going about our routines without interruptions.

- The true strength of these tools lies in their versatility and accessibility – they can be employed whenever needed throughout the day. **When a challenge arises, we can turn to our warrior toolkit, select a relevant tool, and triumph over the obstacle at hand, all while maintaining our forward momentum.**

8 "Starter"

Mental Health Warrior Tools

RECHARGE WITH MINDFULNESS COOKING

GOAL

Slow down your thoughts, recharge your mind & reduce stress. Overall, this tool will strengthen you as a Mental Health Warrior with the practice of Mindfulness!

HOW TO USE THIS SKILL

Mindfulness

Select a simple soup recipe as they work best as soups require a lot of dicing and prep work. This is perfect as we combine the process of cooking with the therapeutic technique of Mindfulness. As the essence of Mindfulness is to focus on what task we are performing, thus limiting, or blocking out the distractions that constantly occur in our technology filled lifestyles. This is to allow our mind to focus on a single task so it can recharge. It is similar to the break we get when we sleep but it can also be performed in small increments throughout the day and provide great results. Additionally, we will find a greater enjoyment in the task at hand, as we take our minds out of multitask mode, and we can have the time to enjoy the process.

The Prep

To focus and gain the best results we want to eliminate as many distractions as possible, so mute your cell phone and turn off the TV. Then while prepping the ingredients for the recipe, focus your mind only on the task at hand. This will give your brain a chance to recharge. You may even be surprised at how calm you can become while cooking. Enjoy the rhythm of this activity, relax in its straightforwardness, and enjoy the success of completing each task. As we quiet our minds and induce a sense of calmness with mindfulness.

Long Term Use

Try to implement this Mental Health Tool into a couple of meals during the week. Or use the technique with your own Meal creation and receive the bonus of self-confidence as you create a unique and tasty meal. Long term use of this tool to provide a calming oasis in your life, will result in greater clarity of thought as you prevent the stress from building up and depleting your energy. This whole process is exhilarating and restorative!

TOP TIPS

- Remove as many distractions as you can (i.e. put cell phone on silence, turn off the TV and set aside the time to cook).
- Pull out all the recipe contents and prepare your workspace as the first step to minimize distractions.
- Focus on each food item as you prepare it, allowing yourself maximum time to concentrate on the task at hand and enjoy the freedom of focus (mindfulness)!

HANDLE A BAD DAY

GOAL

Establish a plan for dealing with a bad day that helps prevent going back to old lifestyle choices. This is a great first attempt at learning to Bend Not Break when challenged by life!

HOW TO USE THIS SKILL

Accept and Prep

Who doesn't have a bad day now and then…no one! But with new lifestyle changes, things can become magnified and soon you are at risk for backsliding! Not something we want to do! So, to be prepared when life throws you a curve ball, we set up this plan. We begin by baking cookies before we are in crisis! Of course, let's be realistic, a few of these delicious cookies may get eaten today but be sure to sock a few of them away. So, whip up a batch of cookies, put them aside with the label "break open when a tough day occurs". At this point we are prepared for when we find ourselves having a bad day with our ready-made Comfort Food.

When Problems Strike

Next time something triggers you and your old habits try to call you back, grab the cookies and take a 5-minute break. Think of the cookies as a bribe to your mind. We are buying some pleasant time to think through what we want to do next. Do we want to retreat from our lifestyle changes, back to all those old problems, or do we want to continue with our progress? Those few minutes will give us a chance to respond not react. Who knew that cookies could be so useful!

Long Term

This may sound like we are planning to have problems or bad days, but nothing is further from the truth. Instead, we are teaching ourselves to learn to live with the normal ups and downs of daily life without Breaking. We are taking steps to start learning to sit with our feelings. Over time we will learn to combine this with the Respond Not React rule to make better choices that keep us on the path to our new life!

TOP TIPS

- When a tough time strikes, we can take some time to enjoy our comfort food and realize that our old lifestyle feelings will pass.
- Use this skill to take a pause, which will give us the power to make choices and respond instead of reacting. Which has just gotten us into more trouble in the past.
- Embrace this Mental Health Tool and start the journey of learning to deal with your feelings!

60 SECOND GRATITUDE LIST

GOAL

Whenever you find yourself feeling depressed about your situation, sad because you do not feel like you are getting anywhere or perhaps teetering on the brink of giving up and returning to your old ways... Pull this tool from your toolbelt and be a Warrior as you re-center you're thinking and find positive energy!

HOW TO USE THIS SKILL

Stop What You are Doing

The most important step, once you realize you are being overwhelmed by negative feelings, is to STOP and take 60 seconds for yourself. The beauty of this skill is it can be interwoven into just about any part of your day. You can take a pause while cooking, at your desk or at home. However, it is best to avoid doing this while driving or if you are in the middle of a conversation with someone, just to be safe and not provoke questions like "Are you all right?" LOL!

Build the List

During your first 30 seconds, quickly run through your day. Did you have a place to sleep? Did you enjoy a good meal? Do you have a car, job, prospects for a job or perhaps you are just starting recovery and just started a plan of action? Did you have the opportunity to work-out today? Have you had the opportunity to make Choices today? Are you simply not following your old habits today (as that is something to be very proud of!) I believe you get the idea and within 30 seconds you will find numerous things you can add to your Gratitude List.

Process the List

Take 30 seconds to process the list in your mind, quickly reviewing each item and recognizing its value. Plus, as you review your list, remember there are a lot of people that would love to have what you just listed in their lives. This is not to make you feel bad, but to help you see the value in each item even if they are still a work in progress! Also, be sure to acknowledge the positive steps you are taking by engaging in this exercise and working to become a... Mental Health Warrior. All amazing results of a 60-second Gratitude list!

TOP TIPS

- First and important step... Recognize when you are being overwhelmed and take a pause.
- Avoid distractions and truly give yourself 60 uninterrupted seconds.
- Make sure to process your list to get the full effect.

FIND PEACE THROUGH YOUR WORKOUT

GOAL

Complete a workout and merge it with the practice of mindfulness. This facilitates a reduction of stress and strengthens your positive mental health!

HOW TO USE THIS SKILL

Head to the Gym

Most people associate the practice of Mindfulness with meditation and envision meditating in a quiet room while chanting "Ommm." While that is one way to practice and achieve a calm state, we are going to use it quite differently. We are going to pull this skill from our toolbelt when you have had a stressful day and/or perhaps anger is threatening to overwhelm your mental health. Instead of letting that happen and perhaps risking the return of old behavior, grab your workout gear and head to the gym.

Focus and Focus

When you get there, get ready to take a new approach for the day. We are going to perform a Mindfulness Workout! As you perform each rep (and set of exercises) instead of thinking about what is stressing or angering you, focus instead on the form of each rep and the action of lifting. While you may say, but I always pay attention to what I'm doing in the gym, the goal is to think and focus on nothing but each rep that you are performing. This does not mean you have to shut off your favorite music, as it can certainly provide motivation and a nice distraction from the noise of the gym. But pay attention to each rep!

The Results

We are working to obtain the results of Mindfulness by using the workout as our point of focus. This will provide you with a respite from racing thoughts, give your emotions a chance to settle and provide psychological benefits as we reduce our stress and anxiety levels. Combined with physical benefits such as increasing your energy from completing a workout. Continued use of this tool will provide amazing mindfulness benefits and provide another tool from your warrior Mental Health Toolbelt!

TOP TIPS

- Remember the focus of the workout IS the workout.
- Stick with your exercise schedule, as we don't want to complicate things, and focus your thoughts on paying attention to the workout.
- Limit Distractions (stay off the phone, avoid extra chatting).

MORNING RESTORATIVE PAUSE

GOAL

Restore a sense of calmness to our thinking, especially when morning business interruptions (waking up and grabbing your phone is most people's first reaction these days) threaten to derail our thinking.

HOW TO USE THIS SKILL

The Reason

There is no perfect pose for your Morning Restorative Pause but I will offer up one that works well. Also, you may chuckle a bit but once you try it, I believe you will find it easy and helpful. Like most people these days I use my phone as an alarm clock, which means I reach for it first thing in the morning. When checking the time, to decide if I can hit the snooze one more time, I see all the pop-up messages on the screen. Texts that came in or notices from programs, good stuff, but it tends to instantly bring you into the day. While it is nice to stay informed this is not the most effective way to start the day. Instead, building in a Morning Restorative Pause is a fantastic way to give your brain a calm starting point and allow for true planning.

The Pose and Action

The pose I take for my restorative break is the Quad Stretch. Start by kneeling on the ground with the tops of your feet flat on the floor. Then lower your butt down onto the top of your heels, keeping your back erect. Now lean back, keeping your back flat (don't let your knees pop up), let your arms stretch out, and feel the big stretch in your legs (quadriceps). Hold that position for up to 2 minutes. In order to help time the hold I brush my teeth with my electric toothbrush which has a 2-minute timer. Plus, brushing your teeth is something that helps you focus as it does not require a lot of concentration. Feel free to chuckle at this point!

Results

The results of incorporating this Restorative Pause into the morning madness will have outstanding benefits. It will provide you with a calm starting point that you can use to start planning your day. It will also allow you to be more focused, as you will have given your brain some time to clear whatever popped up on your phone, or any other numerous attention grabbers that may have occurred. While you may think this is a lot to ask of a simple two-minute break, it is the small changes that can often have the biggest impact!

TOP TIPS

- Limit distractions (don't bring your phone into the bathroom)
- Find a simple activity you can concentrate on.
- Use that activity to help with timing the break.

AROMA THERAPY (COOKING)

GOAL

Use the smell of an all-day cooking recipe to brighten your mood. Also, you will create a delicious recipe which can be used all week in a variety of healthy meals! Big Double Win for a Warrior!

HOW TO USE THIS SKILL

The Recipe

Some of the recipes that are excellent for this skill are Marinara Sauce or any Soup Recipe because you can leave them simmering all day long! This will not burn the sauces and I feel that the longer they cook, the more delicious they become. So, make sure to choose your favorite recipe that is perfect for simmering on the stove or in a slow cooker (crockpot). I find the recipes that simmer the longest will completely infuse your apartment/house with a delicious aroma that will greet you as you enter! Delightful Welcome!

The Action

The action of this skill is fairly easy. Start the recipe and enjoy the aroma. But in reality, what makes this skill so successful is to take a few moments and truly enjoy the aroma every time you are near the kitchen. Do not just smell the food cooking but allow your mind time to process the smell and bring up the thoughts associated with it. It is like a quick trip down memory lane for your mind. The sauce may trigger memories of a great dinner you had with friends, or a summer vacation when you had time to truly savor your meals. These positive experiences are interlocked in your brain with your senses and this skill can help you tap into those feelings.

Results

The results of this skill are twofold. One, throughout the day you can reinforce positive thoughts through enjoying the aroma and associated memories. This will effectively help keep you on track and in times of struggle, can help pull you out. The second benefit is even more tangible. If a day later you find yourself struggling with a challenge, grab the leftovers from this exercise. Then let it reheat on the stove, enjoying the delightful smells and memories that it recalls. This simple tool will allow you to recenter your thoughts and prevent you from being overwhelmed. That is a Mental Health Warrior in action with Soup! MMM!

TOP TIPS

- Pick a sauce recipe that you truly enjoy both the smell and the taste, to double the benefits!
- Consider using a crockpot, that will switch to warm, thus allowing the aroma to continue to fill the room, even when done cooking.

SHARING/SOCIAL INTERACTION FUELED BY COOKIES

GOAL

This tool helps to re-engage with people and stop isolation! All by creating some delicious (and hopefully healthy) treats that can be shared!

HOW TO USE THIS SKILL

Cookie Creation

The first part of this skill involves baking cookies, or any treat that can be easily shared. Find an easy recipe that you enjoy baking and first enjoy the process (bit of mindfulness). Plus find positivity when you pull the tray from the oven and see the delicious treats that you created. Now the tricky part is to remember not to eat all the cookies while they are still warm, or you will be left with nothing for the second part of the skill!

Sharing and Engaging with Friends

This is where the true benefits of the Mental Health Tool really shine. Pack up the cookies that you baked and bring them to a group of people that you may have isolated yourself from when life's challenges were in charge. Understand that this isolation tends to be a defense mechanism and occurs because life's challenges tend to consume our thoughts and they rob us of our energy. But with this tool we change all that by sharing cookies and connecting with people. The cookies are our ice breaker to help us find that common ground and reconnect.to reconnect with people!

Results

The offer of a cookie can have an immediate impact as it shows someone who knows you that you are working on changing your life. Your baking of a simple treat demonstrates you are focusing your energies on a new area. Then making the effort to bring them to someone and sharing them starts the process of reconnecting as you discuss the baking process or even simply what they like in a dessert. This tool helps find a way to get past that awkward first few second and that is absolutely a Mental Health Warrior... finding solutions to challenges!

TOP TIPS

- Pick a recipe that is easy to share (cake can work but cookies are a lot easier to carry!)
- Do not force them on people! Even if someone declines the offer as they do not fit their way of eating, you still can start a conversation. That is our goal, the cookies are just to Break the Ice!
- Offer them in person. While you can leave them for someone, you will miss out on the conversation that can quickly follow the offer.

GRATITUDE THROUGH STRENGTH TRAINING

GOAL

Complete a Strength Training workout while also working an active gratitude session. A great way to re-center your emotional health after a tough day and complete any type of workout. Enjoying the Mental Health benefits of both results!

HOW TO USE THIS SKILL

Workout Plan

Ok, so when workday was plain frustration or the traffic during your commute drove you up the wall. We break out this tool for a good dose of gratitude, but the first step is to make time to get to the gym and select your workout plan. Once you change clothes and suit up, we take a new direction with this tool.

Workout Execution

We follow our workout plan but focus on creating a mental gratitude list as we work on each exercise throughout our entire workout. This is not a hard and fast rule as we don't want to literally stop each rep just because we can't quickly come up with an answer. As that would negate the benefit of sustained activity that is an essential component of the workout. Instead build your list along the flow of the workout. As you liftin weights remember to be grateful that we have a place to work out, time to work out and even grateful that we can lift the amount weight we are currently lifting!

Results

The result of completing your workout with gratitude is a re-centered mind and a sense of calm. I referred to this process as "Iron Therapy", which is a reference to how we dissipate anger or frustration by using the physical challenges to center our thoughts and emotions. Also, when we create and review our gratitude list, we redirect our emotions to a positive direction. For it is incredibly difficult to maintain negative thoughts while compiling a list of all that we can be grateful for. Even if things seem bleak at the beginning of the workout, once you begin to break down your day into small pieces you will see there are lots of things to be grateful for! Be a Mental Health Warrior in action!

TOP TIPS

- Select a plan before you begin the workout, to know what exercises you want to complete and can focus on building your gratitude list.
- Challenge yourself to find at least 2 things to be grateful for during each set of reps.
- Pay attention to form to avoid injury, enjoy your list and if you miscount a few reps, it is ok!

Make those small
changes
at each opportunity

That is what will
transform your life

Mental Health Warrior Each and Every Day

REAL-LIFE
RESULTS

How I used
Mindset Rules

<u>Quick Note to Set the Stage:</u>

Think of using the Mindset Rules as like when you use an app on your phone to get directions. You get the entire route displayed in a nice blue line to your destination.

Plus, you get guided information about what areas have traffic, construction, or accident delays. This allows us to adjust our route, as nothing can ruin a trip faster than endless hours spent sitting in the car going nowhere! That might even lead us to giving up the trip and really going nowhere!

To avoid that scenario, **we use Mindset Rules to map out our course and drive without delays towards building the life we really want!**

MINDSET RULE #2

Respond Not React to
Life's Challenges

Respond Not React to Life's Challenges

Early in my journey of wrestling control of my life from challenges, I discovered that when I learned to Respond Not React, I made better choices. This subtle shift in my approach to problems eventually turned into a critical Mindset Rule, that I as a Mental Health Warrior now use every day!

Pause
This approach is so effective because when we take a pause, of even just a few seconds, we can review our values and ensure the actions that we choose are in alignment with them. That produces vastly superior results than reacting to our challenges and the accompanying emotions.

Evaluate
Now, this does not mean I am now "all-knowing" and never get the wrong answer. But particularly in my case, this new approach keeps any missteps as small fires which are quickly extinguished. Whereas previously, each decision was like throwing gasoline onto an already out of control bonfire that threatened to engulf many small nearby villages. And then I spent the majority of my time pulling things out of the fire, which was no way to live!

Keep Moving Forward
Today this simple pause returns amazing results and has become second nature when challenges arise. Which they still do as that is just the nature of life, but when we stay in control with our responses…then we get results and triumph over any challenge that life throws our way.

That is a Mental Health Warrior in Action!

A Pause is not just Stillness,

but a wealth of Time for our brains to

align our actions with our Values,

formulate effective decisions,

all while Moving Forward without missing a Beat

...Bruce

MINDSET RULE #6

Forgive Yourself for Not Knowing,
the things you Know Now

Forgive Yourself for Not Knowing,
the things you Know Now

This is one of those sentences that you need to read several times for it sounds so simple on the surface, but the powerful meaning is sitting just below it. Go ahead and re-read the rule, I will wait.

Focus on Today

Ok, time's up! When we learn how to handle a challenge in life better, we are excited. But then, right on its heels comes the twist... why didn't I do that years ago?! Yup, it's common, because we know when we have something figured out, it now looks easy. I mean the solution was right there, what am I an idiot for not seeing it?

Give Yourself Break for Yesterday

A resounding NO! First, we must understand that our life today is not exactly the same as it was years ago. There are a million variables in each day and the odds are almost zero that everything is the same. In my case, my Bipolar was untreated, because I didn't even know I had it, it was undiagnosed. Now I like to think that I am fairly intelligent, but to be honest the reality is that we can never know everything. So, should I punish myself for things unknown? No, so I need to cut myself a break on this one!

Apply the Lessons and Revel in New You

But the most important message that this rule brings to light is that we have learned something new about ourselves or how to handle Life's challenges. It is imperative that we do not minimize or take away from this achievement. As the past has already happened, and we cannot change it. But we can apply that new knowledge to today, make changes today and enjoy the results of a new tomorrow.

So be a Mental Health Warrior and with this rule stop spinning your achievements to the negative! They are Positive!

In order to be Happy in today,
we need to forgive ourselves for what has
occurred in the past.

For although the past has propelled us into this new future
and for that we can thank it.

We owe it no energy from today!

...Bruce

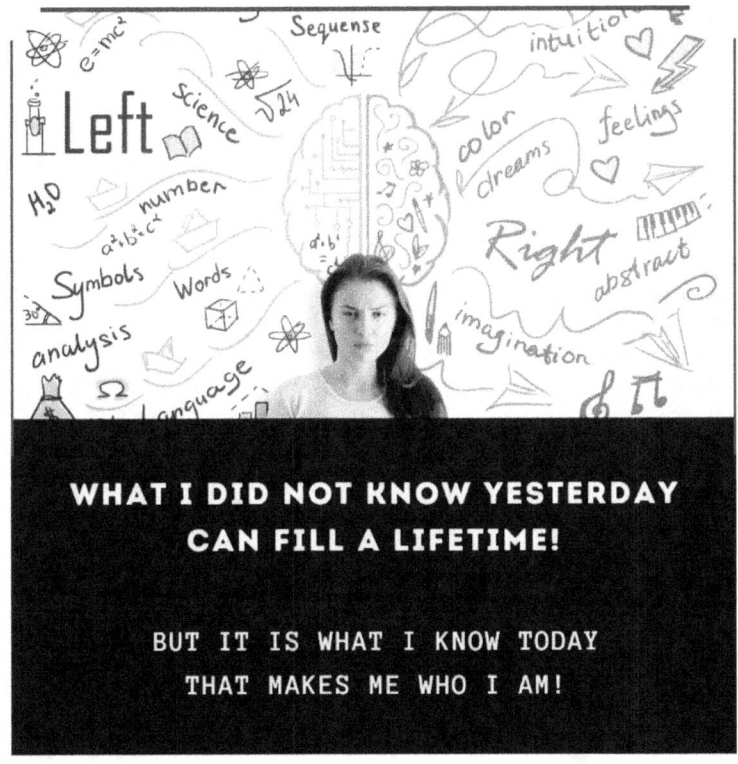

WAIT, STOP!

NEVER FORGET...

Mindset Rule #10 – Have Fun!

Mindset Rule #10 — Have Fun!

Yes, changing our life is serious, hard work and requires dedication, but there is a common pitfall we need to be aware of. We can become so serious that even when we make progress on changing the direction of our life, we just do not seem to enjoy it. We are so caught up in the process and ensuring that we stay true to our new way of living that we lose sight of the reason we started the whole process…

We want to <u>Live this amazing New Life</u>!

The absolute best way I found for avoiding this situation is never forget… Mindset Rule #10 — Have Fun!

Reward
It reminds me that we are allowed and encouraged to have fun during the day. As it is both the reward, we get for taking charge of our mental health, as well as the motivation to continue taking action each day.

New Reward
Now, I will leave the definitions and the choice of activities that are fun left to you. But always remember that when life's challenges ran the show, we most likely never got this benefit. I certainly know that was my experience. That is why today we must never minimize that fun in life is one of the great rewards of our new way of living.

Reward Each Day
Today I incorporate Mindset Rule #10 into each day. Even if it is just 20 minutes playing a video game or simply having the time to cook a new recipe. Now that is a far cry from my past when I spent most of time going from crisis to crisis! Today I am a Warrior who kicks b#tt and has fun.

That is a very cool combo you can have as a Warrior!

Fun is an experience that as a kid we reveled in,
but as we became adults, it got lost along the way.

Perhaps it is the depth of our experiences,
or their serious nature that takes away this joy.

But when we regain control of our life,
we are again rewarded
with the truly joyful experience of having FUN!

...Bruce

EVEN MORE VICTORIES!

Mental Health Warrior vs Anger

Anger is one of the emotions that seems to rear its head early in our journey of regaining control of the direction of our life from life's challenges. We may be mad at the situation we find ourselves in, mad at ourselves for letting our problems control us and overall, just plain mad that we have these problems! This places us in a precarious position, for often the most trivial things will cause us to explode, as we are already on edge.

I personally found that anger was one of the triggers that could easily lead me crawling back into the damn circle. Someone cuts me off in traffic, a problem with finances or I would decide on how to handle a challenge only to find it was ineffective... Yup, you guessed it, mad for the rest of the day and very easy to slide back into old behaviors!

Not Good at all! But then I realized that I needed to put being a Mental Health Warrior into action… I needed to learn how to Bend Not Break when challenges made me angry. This approach allowed me to shortcut and negate the power that anger had on my day… and that made a world of difference in how each day turned out!

Center Yourself

My initial approach is to use Mental Health Tools to prepare myself before even starting an activity. This results in entering situations ready and with tools to adjust as needed.

For example, I center myself and prepare for driving, running errands or even going to the gym by taking just a brief pause to remind myself of how far I have come from my problems. Then if I experience challenges while driving – they remain just that - minor challenges that I can easily defeat!

Sure, I may still get frustrated with the driving or traffic, I mean I am human after all. But the key difference is none of these events light the bonfire of anger. Nope, they are just small smoldering embers for a few minutes, and they are quickly extinguished! That makes for a lot smoother day!

How we Respond to Anger

Now let's be honest, sometimes we find ourselves in much bigger challenges and we just get angry! This will happen as life is not perfect and there are things that we cannot control. Ok, but then what do we do? Here is the secret... it is how we respond to these situations that determines how they turn out. Will they destroy everything we worked for, or can we use them constructively?

This is where I also tap into my Values and use them to maintain the direction I have set for my life. For example, when it rained for 3 days straight and flooded the basement, or when the car we had just bought, less than a week later got backed into while in a parking lot... old reaction was to go ballistic and of course in my case, rant and rave, ruin the day and then use this as an excuse to go back to old behavior.

But no longer, for I manage the situation! First by understanding that it is ok to get angry when something is truly worth getting upset about. Then with that understanding, I renewed my commitment to the value I place on embracing my new way of living. Yes, that new mindset where I refuse to let life's challenge control the direction of my life.

Take Action

I use a Mental Health Tool breathing exercise to calm down and then from this calm, centered place, I work to resolve the situation. In the examples above, I firmly stated my case to our home insurance representative and explained the full situation to the police officer at the accident scene. Much to my surprise... people stepped up to help me fix the situation. For I was not attacking the world, yelling and screaming, but looking for an answer which they were happy to provide.

This new approach is amazing because it negates the anger and leaves me able to continue with the day. Actually, truth be told, I felt so proud of myself that the rest of the week was filled with Positivity. All of this made possible by being a... Mental Health Warrior in action!

Controlled Action results in a Solution...
No more powerful words ever spoken!

Mental Health Warrior vs Depression

The simplest description I have of depression is loss of hope. Whether this is due to a mental health challenge, an alcoholism problem or any other life challenge, the results all end up in the same place... despair and loss of hope. This is an extremely tough spot to be in and there is no single fix as each situation is different.

But how we respond to depression as a Mental Health Warrior is what will make you successful in overcoming this challenge. The power to do this lies squarely within the values we set, the mindset we build and the mental health tools on our toolbelt.

First Level of Depression

I like to break down my responses to depression into two levels. In the first level, depression is just looking for a way into my day. It has not firmly planted itself into the day and the goal is to minimize its power and kick it to the curb.

I personally found that using a mental health tool based on using music is particularly helpful in accomplishing this task. To be prepared for these situations, I created two playlists, one with thought provoking songs and the other with powerful uplifting music. Then when something starts to bring me down, I stop, grab my headphones and depending on my mood I blast the music playlist.

The reason I have two types of playlists, is sometimes the situation causing depression is very serious and I employ the playlist with song lyrics that remind me about certain things I value. For example, the REM song "Everybody Hurts" conveys the message to me that life is precious, and we need to keep moving forward with our new way of living, even when we feel pain. The other list, believe it or not, is classical songs that just reverberate with energy. Try listening to the William Tell Overture or Wagner's Ride of the Valkyries and not be energized.

The power of the symphonic music will almost lift you right out of your seat. This combination of tools and values do an amazing job at stopping depression in its tracks!

Second Level

Now that works great for the first level of depression, but when it reaches the second level it usually is entrenched in the day. This is the result of more serious challenges rearing their heads and demanding attention.

In my 2nd year of embracing sobriety and managing my Bipolar way of thinking, the house of cards that we had built with our rental properties collapsed. Yes, partly a result of the real estate crash but largely due to actions taken when I let my life's challenges run the show with abandon. Initially we tried selling several properties to right the ship, but it was too much, and we had no option left but to declare bankruptcy.

Honestly, I thought this would be a death blow, figuratively and literally, for everything was lost. But I dug deep, embraced my new values, and clung to them with fervor.

My New Values

My relationships with my friends and family were more important than possessions. I also realized that a big house and all the time I had spent taking care of it was keeping me from things that I really valued. Essentially, I no longer wanted to be defined by material goods we owned but by the person I was and interests I pursued.

Yes, that was a terrifying proposition for I had never attempted this in the past. But I took the leap as I had worked very hard to identify my values and they felt solid! Amazingly enough, the ROI (return on investment) began almost immediately.

By leaning on my values, I found support to make tough decisions. I also found the power of using Mental Health Tools to manage the challenges that occur almost daily. The result of this combination was the ability to take painful steps needed to eventually get through this process and emerge still in control of my life!

There is a Way Out

Suffice it to say, it was not an easy path, and I am not proud of having to declare bankruptcy! But using Mindset Rules to prepare for each day, Mental Health Tools to triumph over the day's challenges and keeping my actions in alignment with my Values I emerged from this challenge.

But the truly amazing thing is that today, discussing this serious challenge does not bring about depression but further demonstrates to me the power of being a Mental Health Warrior and our ability to find triumph over the most serious of life's challenges! Thus, providing a path out of depression and back into the light of the day!

Mental Health Warrior vs Anxiety/Stress

Anxiety can cause stress and when we are stressed, we fuel our anxiety. That is the situation that I found myself in most days when life's challenges had all the power over my life.

For me personally it was a non-stop barrage, if my bipolar thinking was not in charge then my alcoholism was seeking control of the day. Or if I managed to push these to a secondary position, I was often overwhelmed at work with stress over even the smallest meeting or project. I just could not seem to find a way that worked to handle the stress and anxiety filled days. But I am here today and can say that life today is very different!

Stress and anxiety are still present but by looking inward, I found how to manage them, negate their power, and keep them in their place! That has produced amazing new results!

Values Set Direction

Now as Stress and Anxiety cover a vast area in my life, I use several methods to address them. First and foremost, when I took the time to identify what I value in my life and allowed it to set the direction, I removed a lot of stress from my life.

The best analogy I can think of, is I stepped off the "hamster wheel" in the chase of material goods. No, I did not decide to live in a hut, but I did realize how much money and time I was pouring into things that brought no real meaning or happiness to my life. Funny enough, as a by-product, I found that the items I did acquire held more meaning and brought real happiness to my life. Probably because they were part of each day instead of just piling up somewhere in the house!

Mindset Rules

Next, I needed an approach for the other areas in my life, such as work or my generalized anxiety disorder, where I just worry excessively about everything. And I do mean everything! I started incorporating several of the Mindset Rules into my daily life. If a mistake occurred, I embraced Mindset Rule #5 – Do Not Expect or Demand Perfection. This allowed me to direct my energy back into finding a solution and not ruminating on the failure.

That subtle shift in thinking made all the difference in the world. As I worked to find the right answers for my life, I now looked on a misstep as a learning experience. Yes, as crazy as it sounds, you can place them in the bucket of things that didn't work but inspired me to try... and that brought me success!

With that success, I then bundled two Mindset Rules, (#2 - Respond Not React) & (#7 - Work on the things that you can control and let go of the rest) to overcome the anxiety and stress that I found in other areas of my life. It took, and still takes, work each day to embrace these two rules but they keep me moving forward. Together they have taught me that when anxiety rises if I take that brief pause, I can not only respond but I can evaluate the seriousness of the situation.

Most of the time, I find I am causing a lot of the stress myself. Imagine that, me causing myself problems. A truth that sounds funny even now writing it but one that was unfortunately so true. But now I have a new mindset where I do not seek perfection but results. Again, a mindset shift that keeps me moving forward each day, triumphing over my challenges, and always remaining in control of the direction of my life.

New Perspective

I find my new approach now contains several ways to get to a solution. Many times, what I am obsessing about is just not that important. For example, I bumped the car door with my bag and put a minor scratch in it, I forgot socks for my workout, I cooked a recipe, and it came out less than stellar... oops, not perfect but now relegated to where they belong, minor missteps.

My other approach on Stress and Anxiety is that we must be realistic as we will not be able to banish them completely from our life. But we can triumph over them as a Mental Health Warrior and that is extremely important.

When we stay in control of our emotions during challenges in which we have little or no control, then we have a Winning Plan!

WARRIOR SECRETS

(No Secret Handshake but Still good stuff!)

MENTAL HEALTH WARRIORS
ARE COMPLEX

Mental Health Warriors are Complex

We have just covered but a brief sampling of the challenges in my life, but the results are clear…

Become a Mental Health Warrior
and
You can triumph over your Life's Challenges!

Complexity Equals Power

I say this because I have learned, much to my surprise, that being a Mental Health Warrior is complex and that much of the power comes from this complexity. We set the direction for our life by identifying our Values. We embrace Mindset Rules to help us keep our emotions centered during the day. Then we add in an almost unlimited number of Mental Health Tools to defeat the challenges of the day.

This all takes place under the umbrella of being a Mental Health Warrior and the power this complexity brings to our life.

Don't Forget

Our creed of "Bend Not Break" plays a big part in my triumphing over my life's challenge and honestly adds to the warrior's complex power! Demonstrated by the ability to never lose forward momentum while making slow but steady progress in managing and becoming comfortable in my emotions.

Today, rather than throwing me off my path, they empower me to embrace a new life and strengthen my power to set the direction for my life and continue on that path!

So, let's wrap up this warrior secret with one thought…

COMPLEXITY CREATES POWER, EMBRACE IT!

Life's Challenges lose their power when they

encounter a Mental Health Warrior,

with their direction set by their Values,

the Mindset to succeed,

and the Tools to make it Happen.

So today, be a Warrior,

each and every day,

reveling in the results of this complex approach

that builds your path to triumph!

...Bruce

Mental health

is a

Learned Skill

Mental Health as a Learned Skill:
Empowering Your Mental Health Warrior Journey

In life, we often find ourselves entangled in a web of emotions, grappling with the challenges that come our way. For many years, I navigated through the labyrinth of anxiety disorders and bipolar thinking, seeking solace in short-term solutions that offered fleeting relief but brought new problems into my life.

Little did I know that a profound revelation awaited me—a revelation that mental health is not an elusive concept reserved for a select few, but a learned skill accessible to everyone, regardless of where they are in life or in their struggles.

Embracing this truth allowed me to understand the power that comes with this belief and taught me several lessons that emphasized how my Mental Health Warrior power would grow.

I am Not Powerless

The first lesson that dawned upon me was the realization that I am not powerless in the face of life's challenges and the accompanying emotions. Previously, I struggled to manage the tumultuous waves of anxiety and bipolar thoughts, leading me down paths of temporary respite that only exacerbated my problems. This epiphany—that mental health is a skill to be acquired—was transformative and empowering. It marked the beginning of my journey towards mastering the art of managing emotions and harnessing that power to triumph over life's adversities.

I Can Grow my Power

The second lesson I learned was equally profound: viewing mental health as a learned skill allowed me to grow into a mental health warrior. No longer did I need to fear the daunting task of embracing my emotions today; instead, I could embark on a journey of gradual learning and self-discovery. Similar to acquiring a new skill at work or in school, there was a "grace period" that offered respite and permission to learn over time.

This perspective alleviated the pressure, granting me the freedom to evolve each day, fortifying my warrior strength, and honing the ability to confront even more formidable emotions and life challenges. It was a double win—evidence that, as mental health warriors, we possess the resilience to handle any curveball life throws our way.

We all have this Power
The third and perhaps most liberating lesson was the recognition that mental health, being a learned skill, is accessible to everyone. It is not a mystical concept reserved for a privileged few; rather, it is a power inherent in our shared humanity and the emotions we all experience.

This revelation swung open the door to a new paradigm, dispelling the notion that mental health is an exclusive master program. Instead, it affirmed that each of us, by virtue of being human, is inherently qualified to learn how to manage our emotions, extract lessons from them, and apply that newfound power to triumph over life's challenges.

Now, Go Forth and Triumph

USE THE
WARRIOR PRINCIPLES DAILY

Mental Health Warrior Principles

I believe that many times when we struggle with any of life's challenges, the biggest threat we face is that they leave us feeling powerless. Which often means that we do not even want to take any action for it just seems hopeless. That means we will not get to experience the amazing results and motivation that I just spoke about in the last chapter. Our mindset has defeated us before we even give the warrior tools a chance!

The Solution
But as I have personally experienced this, and saw my life go nowhere, I found a solution in this non-traditional tool – **The Warrior Principles** – that we can use to negate what challenges are telling us and spur action, resulting in triumph!

What Are They
The Warrior Principles outline what is possible when we become mental health warriors and, in many cases, outline how we will achieve them (the game plan).

Think about them as the world's greatest pep-talk to use when life's challenges are whispering in our ears that we cannot win. But instead, with a printed copy in our hand and in just under 2 minutes, we can review this list to remind ourselves of the power we have as mental health warriors.

That is why I like to call the warrior principles your:

All-In-One Warrior <u>Pre-Game Speech</u> and <u>Game Plan</u>!

How do they Work?

Much of its power comes from seeing all of the warrior powers together, which is why I strongly suggest printing out a copy of the Warrior Principles. For there is a strong psychological impact in seeing that becoming a mental health warrior has a vast positive impact on all areas of your life.

And that serves to negate the thought that we are powerless before life's challenges. As a matter of fact, that point is so powerful that I made it one of the warrior principles, so that we never forget this point!

Next, that piece of paper holds the outline for how a warrior lives each day, which ties into our values. Think of the principles as the power to choose how you want to live your life.

How I Use Them

In my case this meant I decided to be in charge and while I cannot make bipolar disappear from my life, today I have the tools to manage wherever it sends me on the emotional spectrum.

I also view the principles as the outline for how I moved forward from using alcohol each day to hide from my emotions. For it provides me with reminders that I have the power today when I ally with my emotions to actually live life!

Best Used Every Day

So, while they are at the end of this book, I believe we will all benefit from using them every day. For they give you both guidance and motivation…

making them a powerful tool in your warrior's arsenal!

MENTAL HEALTH WARRIOR PRINCIPLES

1. Mental Health (emotions) is a strength not a weakness.

2. Emotions hold significant power because they are intertwined with and affect every aspect of our lives.

3. Mental Health Warrior is comfortable with the full spectrum of emotions, which empowers the full life experience.

4. When we manage our emotions, we can take the necessary steps to overcome any challenges that life throws our way.

5. You are not defined or limited by your life's challenges.

6. Talking about your emotions is one of the most powerful and effective weapons to strengthen your mental health.

7. Move past the past by applying the lesson of yesterday to the actions of today.

8. Emotions can be Complex, but Solutions don't have to be.

9. Never let life's challenges tell you there are no answers.

10. Life should not be defined or consumed by our challenges or the solutions, it is meant for living. Live Life!

11. Mental Health is a learned skill, which means the future is yours to build.

12. Mental Health Warriors confront life's challenges as they have the skills and tools to triumph over them.

13. By becoming a Mental Health Warrior, we establish a solid foundation that enables us to seek help for more complex or challenging issues.

14. Everyone has the power within themselves to be a Mental Health Warrior and emerge victorious!

15. New Mindset - New Life - New Future

Warrior Principles are Straight forward in presentation,
but just like in a game of Chess, each piece plays a Role.

Some are used every day,
while others are saved for those big moves.

But in Life, as in Chess,
You cannot triumph without the Power
that comes when all of the piece's work Together!

THE RESULTS OF

BEING A

MENTAL HEALTH WARRIOR

The Result: An Amazing Life!

I hope you have enjoyed this journey but there is one more point I want to bring to your attention. Hey, I saw that... don't roll your eyes, this is important!

Plus, I would be remiss if I didn't leave you with one more philosophical thought to ponder. Ok so here goes...

When all your energy is focused on a solution,

it will engulf your day, your life and

eventually consume every minute of your life.

But we will not be fearful,

as it imparts a life so amazing,

that you will never desire to look or go back!

That is my philosophical way of saying, as a Mental Health Warrior, you will live a life where you are comfortable with the full spectrum of emotions, have the power to triumph over any challenges in life and the power build the life you really want!

Or even more bluntly stated:

When you can handle a shit day in life,
then anything is possible!

No matter what definition you like, they all mean the same thing:

Become a Mental Health Warrior,

Live an Amazing Life!

Life should not be defined or consumed by your challenges, or the solutions, it is meant for living...

LIVE LIFE!

LIVE THE LIFE YOU WANT

BECOME A MENTAL HEALTH WARRIOR

Mental Health Warrior Book Series

"Real-Life Solutions and Results,
Fueled by the Power of Your Mental Health"

I triumphed over Bipolar, Alcoholism & Anxiety Disorder
by becoming a Mental Health Warrior

20 Truths about Mental Health that Everyone Needs to Hear

53 Mindset Rules of a Mental Health Warrior

One Bag Life of a Mental Health Warrior

Euphoria of Today

3 Food Rules of a Mental Health Warrior

Mental Health Warriors Journal - Embrace Your Emotions

84 Mental Health Warrior Tools

Thoughts to Ponder on Mental Health Disorders

(Paperback, Hardback, and eBooks available on Amazon)